Fitz and Will

The Cambridge Cats

The Graduation Adventure

This Fitz & Will adventure belongs to

....

Look out for us!

Written by Laura Robson Brown
Illustrated by Jia Han
Devised by Katherine Mann

One day, if you wander through old Cambridge streets,
Exploring the beautiful places,
You'll find a museum, the famous Fitzwilliam,
And look – two pussycat faces.

By the great lions the Cambridge Cats live,
Look closely, you'll probably see them.
Upon the stone paws, Fitz and Will watch the tours
Taking visitors round the museum.

Fancy-Foot Fitz loves footwear to bits
And will follow the best shoes through town.
High heels, ribbon bows,
Sparkly boots, pointy toes,
In orange, green, pink, blue or brown.

Whisker-Twitch Will likes to stay by her side,
But wonderful food fills his dreams.
Jam doughnuts and cake,
Ice-cream with a flake,
Or even some old custard creams.

One morning, as Cambridge wakes up for the day,
Fitz and Will set off as a pair,
Past school children, bicycles, scooters and tricycles,
Into the Market Square.

The stalls are just opening, fruit piled high,
The cats stop to rest on the fountain,
Around them sweet smells and the chime of church bells,
Then Will spots a big waffle mountain.

He's off in a flash to the sprinkles and syrup,
Sending some strawberries scattering.
Whoops! Slipping on jam, he falls into a pram
And the baby wakes up with the clattering.

Fancy-Foot Fitz meanwhile happily potters
Past flower stalls, tables and chairs;
Fresh bread, stinky cheese, hot coffees and teas,
A huge pile of apples and pears.

Then Fitz catches sight of some beautiful shoes:
Hot pink, with a blue velvet bow.
She happily dances and pounces and prances
And follows wherever they go.

THE GUILDHALL

Where has she gone? Will is lost without Fitz,
So he searches her favourite places.
He knocks down the stand of a busking brass band,
Then at last finds her chasing some laces.

With a pitter-pat patter the cats leave the Square,
Weaving their way down the street.
They jump and they run, then for even more fun
They leap on a bicycle seat.

Whizzing past shoppers and open-topped buses,
They wave, and then they are gone.
By the Round Church, both cats make a lurch
For the towering gate of St John's.

Cobbles and paths and perfect green grass,
A huge tent with tables and chairs.
The Cambridge Cats gaze as the waiters take trays
Of iced cupcakes and chocolate eclairs.

Graduation
Guests
This Way

The Graduation feast makes Will's whiskers twitch,
But Fitz leads him out of his dreaming.
Will keeps looking back, so walks right in the track
Of a trolley with sheets stacked for cleaning.

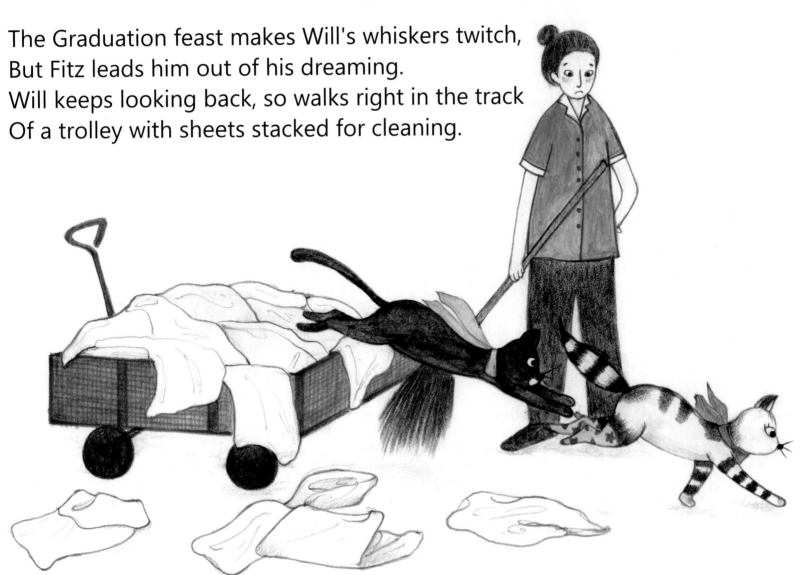

They scamper and scatter and pitter-pat-patter
Away, as the cross cleaner wails,
'You mischievous pests! Just look at this mess!'
But she barely sees more than their tails.

The cats have escaped – they run through a cloister,
And out of a gateway they fly,
Across huge, green lawns, past students in gowns,
Then, before them, the old Bridge of Sighs.

Splashes and squeals from the punts on the river,
Fitz and Will leap off the wall,
The camera clicks as the cats join the mix,
Nearly causing some students to fall.

The students line up and begin to process,
The cats, intrigued, follow on.
Fitz spots some great shoes, there's no time to lose,
Uh-oh, in a flash she is gone!

Will worries and flurries,
He cannot see Fitz,
He's lost without her once more.

Scampering through flowers for what feels like hours,
He passes the Master's front door.

Fitz, meanwhile, is racing ahead,
She's following fancy-foot feet.
The students don't stop, so she runs to keep up
And discovers she's back in the street.

St John's now behind him, Will almost forgets
He's alone when he spies some ice-cream,
But then hurries and scurries, poor Will – how he worries,
It's surely a very bad dream.

Then look – far ahead, Will sees all the students,
Perhaps Fitz has followed them there?
Oh, what a disaster, he runs a bit faster
To find her, he's no idea where.

With a scamper and scatter and pitter-pat-patter
Will chases the black and white gowns,
A path lined with trees runs through Gonville and Caius,
Then a tall gate with views of the town.

No sign of his friend, oh where could she be?
Will climbs up the great Gate of Honour.
Then, over the wall, there are gowns after all,
Perhaps he will now come upon her.

At last he sees Fitz! She's there at a party,
Excited, Will leaps off the gate.
He rushes to find her, then creeps up behind her
And pounces, before it's too late.

Together again, the adventure now over,
The cats leave the party behind.
The end of the day means it's time to make way
Back home again, tails intertwined.

Over old cobbles, past grand crested gates,
Fitz and Will trot down the street,